SHAPE LAND
FIGURALANDIA

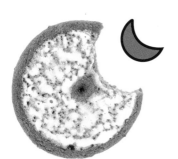

Grow a bilingual vocabulary by:

- **Looking** at pictures and words
- **Talking** about what you see
- **Touching** and naming objects
- **Using** questions to extend learning...
  Ask questions that invite children
  to share information.
  Begin your questions with words like...
  who, what, when, where and how.

Aumenta tu vocabulario bilingüe:

- **Mirando** las imágenes y las palabras
- **Hablando** de lo que ves
- **Tocando** y nombrando los objetos
- **Usando** preguntas para aumentar el aprendizaje...
  Usa preguntas que inviten a los niños a compartir
  la información.
  Empieza tus frases con el uso de estas palabras:
  ¿quién? ¿qué? ¿cuándo? ¿dónde? y ¿cómo?

These books support a series of educational games by Learning Props.
Estos libros refuerzan una serie de juegos educativos desarrollados por Learning Props.
Learning Props, L.L.C., P.O. Box 774, Racine, WI 53401-0774
1-877-776-7750   www.learningprops.com

Created by **Creado por:** Bev Schumacher, Learning Props, L.L.C.
Graphic Design **Diseñadora gráfica:** Bev Kirk
Images **Fotos:** Hemera Technologies Inc., Matthew 25 Ministries, Bev Kirk
Spanish Translation **Traducción al español:** Elaine St. John-Lagenaur, Myriam Sosa, Rosana Sartirana
Translation Consultant **Asesor de traducción:** Luis Pinto

Library of Congress Control Number 2003097927   ISBN 978-0-9741549-2-3

circle
el círculo

clock
el reloj

cookie
la galleta

ring
el anillo

cup and saucer
la taza y el plato

orange slice
la rodaja
de naranja

compact disc (CD)
el disco compacto

button
el botón

tire
la llanta

traffic light
el semáforo

coins
las monedas

square
el cuadrado

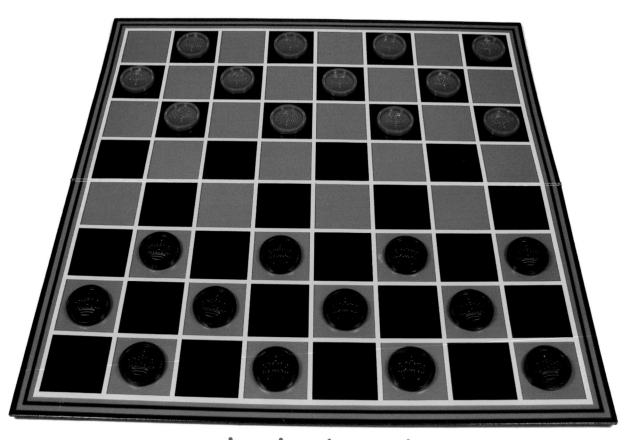

checkerboard
el tablero de damas

flag
la bandera/
el banderín

button
el botón

bread
el pan

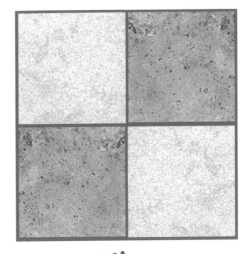

tiles
las baldosas

picture frame
el portarretrato

triangle
el triángulo

roof
el techo

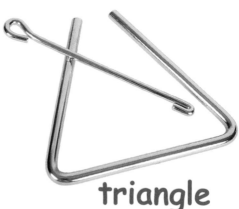

triangle
el triángulo

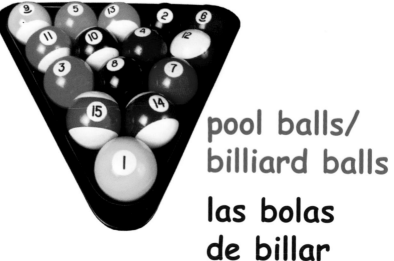

pool balls/
billiard balls

las bolas
de billar

sailboat
el velero/
el barco de vela

quilt
la colcha

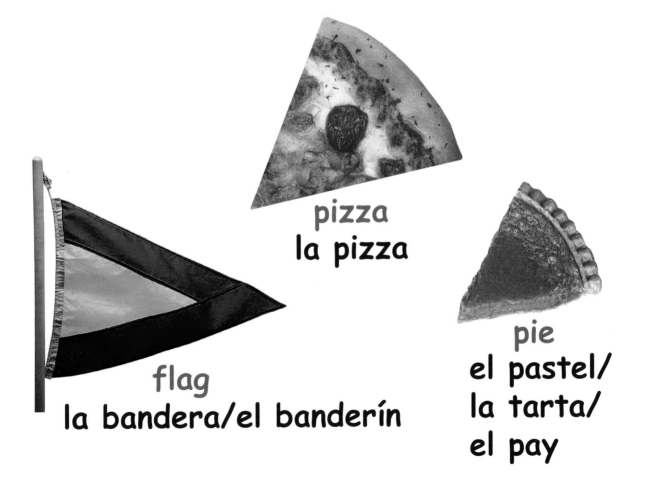

pizza
la pizza

flag
la bandera/el banderín

pie
**el pastel/
la tarta/
el pay**

rectangle
el rectángulo

notebook
el cuaderno

bricks
los ladrillos

suitcase
la maleta

pillow
el cojín/
el almohadón

window
la ventana

money
el dinero/los billetes

book
el libro

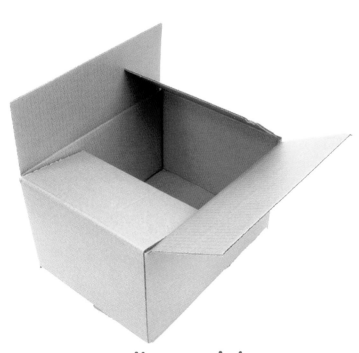

cardboard box
la caja de cartón

oval
el óvalo

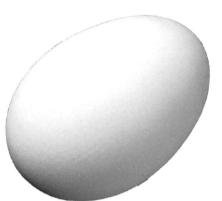

egg
el huevo

picture
frame
el portarretrato

tray
**la charola/
la bandeja**

heart
el corazón

card
la carta

necklace
el collar

basket
la canasta

candies
los dulces

strawberries
las fresas

pentagon
el pentágono

house
la casa

crosswalk sign
la señal de cruce escolar

soccer ball
el balón de fútbol/
la pelota de fútbol

octagon
el octágono

eight sided bowl
el tazón de ocho lados

stop sign
la señal de alto

crescent
la media luna

moon
la luna

banana
el plátano/
la banana

cookies
las galletas

star
la estrella

starfish
la estrella
de mar

T-shirt
la camiseta

diamond
el diamante/el rombo

kite
la cometa/
el papalote

birdhouse
la casita
para pájaros

signs
las señales

volume
el volumen

pyramid
la pirámide

cylinder
el cilindro

cube
el cubo

sphere
la esfera

cone
el cono

balls
las pelotas

yarn
el hilo/la lana/
el estambre

party hat
el gorrito de fiesta

tree
el árbol

blocks
los bloques

clock
el reloj

dice
los dados

can
la lata

find the shapes
busca las figuras

pronunciation
la pronunciación

circle / **sur**-kuhl / el círculo / ayl **seer**-koo-loh

cone / **kohn** / el cono / ayl **koh**-noh

crescent / **kress**-uhnt / la media luna / lah **may**-deeah **loo**-nah

cube / **kyoob** / el cubo / ayl **koo**-boh

cylinder / **sil**-uhn-dur / el cilindro / ayl see-**leen**-droh

diamond / **dye**-muhnd / el diamante, el rombo / ayl dee-ah-**mahn**-tay, ayl **rrohm**-boh

heart / **hart** / el corazón / ayl koh-rah-**sohn**

octagon / **ok**-tuh-gon / el octágono / ayl ohk-**tah**-goh-noh

oval / **oh**-vuhl / el óvalo / ayl **oh**-vah-loh

pentagon / **pen**-tuh-gon / el pentágono / ayl payn-**tah**-goh-noh

pyramid / **pihr**-uh-mid / la pirámide / lah pee-**rah**-mee-day

rectangle / **rek**-tang-guhl / el rectángulo / ayl rrayk-**tahn**-goo-loh

sphere / **sfihr** / la esfera / lah ays-**fay**-rah

square / **skwair** / el cuadrado / ayl koo-ah-**drah**-doh

star / **star** / la estrella / lah ays-**tray**-yah

triangle / **trye**-ang-guhl / el triángulo / ayl tree-**ahn**-goo-loh

volume / **vol**-yuhm / el volumen / ayl voh-**loo**-mayn

balls / **bawls** / las pelotas / lahs pay-**loh**-tahs

banana / buh-**na**-nuh / el plátano, la banana / ayl **plah**-tah-noh, lah bah-**nah**-nah

basket / **bass**-kit / la canasta / lah kah-**nahs**-tah

birdhouse / **bird**-houss / la casita para pájaros / lah kah-**see**-tah **pah**-rah **pah**-hah-rohs

blocks / **bloks** / los bloques / lohs **bloh**-kays

book / **buk** / el libro / ayl **lee**-broh

bread / **bred** / el pan / ayl pahn

bricks / **briks** / los ladrillos / lohs lah-**dree**-yohs

button / **buht**-uhn / el botón / ayl boh-**tohn**

can / **kan** / la lata / lah **lah**-tah

candies / **kan**-deez / los dulces / lohs **dool**-says

card / **kard** / la carta / lah **kahr**-tah

cardboard box / **kard**-bord **boks** / la caja de cartón / lah **kah**-hah day kahr-**tohn**

checkerboard / **chek**-ur-bord / el tablero de damas / ayl tah-**blay**-roh day **dah**-mahs

clock / **klok** / el reloj / ayl ray-**lohgh**

coins / **koins** / las monedas / lahs moh-**nay**-dahs

compact disc (CD) / kuhm-**pakt disk** / el disco compacto / ayl **dees**-koh kohm-**pahk**-toh

cookie(s) / **kuk**-ee(s) / la (las) galleta(s) / lah(lahs) gah-**yay**-tah(s)

crosswalk sign / **krawss**-wawk **sine** / la señal de cruce escolar / lah say-**nyahl** day **kroo**-say ays-koh-**lahr**

cup and saucer / **kuhp and saw**-sur / la taza y el plato / lah **tah**-sah ee ayl **plah**-toh

dice / **disse** / los dados / lohs **dah**-dohs

egg / **eg** / el huevo / ayl oo-**ay**-voh

eight sided bowl / **ate sided bohl** / el tazón de ocho lados / ayl tah-**sohn** day **oh**-shoh **lah**-dohs

flag / **flag** / la bandera, el banderín / lah bahn-**day**-rah, ayl bahn-day-**reen**

house / **houss** / la casa / lah **kah**-sah

kite / **kite** / la cometa, el papalote / lah koh-**may**-tah, ayl pah-pah-**loh**-tay

money / **muhn**-ee / el dinero, los billetes / ayl dee-**nay**-roh, lohs bee-**yay**-tays

moon / **moon** / la luna / lah **loo**-nah

necklace / **nek**-liss / el collar / ayl koh-**yahr**

notebook / **noht**-buk / el cuaderno / ayl koo-ah-**dayr**-noh

orange slice / **or**-inj **slisse** / la rodaja de naranja / lah roh-**dah**-hah day nah-**rahn**-hah

party hat / **par**-tee **hat** / el gorrito de fiesta / ayl goh-**rree**-toh day fee-**ays**-tah

picture frame / **pik**-chur **fraym** / el portarretrato / ayl pohr-tah-rray-**trah**-toh

pie / **pye** / el pastel, la tarta, el pay / ayl pahs-**tayl**, lah **tahr**-tah, ayl **pah**-ee

pillow / **pil**-oh / el cojín, el almohadón / ayl koh-**heen**, ayl ahl-moh-ah-**dohn**

pizza / **peet**-suh / la pizza / lah **pee**-sah

pool balls, billiard balls / **pool bawls**, **bil**-yurd **bawls** / las bolas de billar / lahs **boh**-lahs day bee-**yahr**

quilt / **kwilt** / la colcha / lah **kohl**-shah

ring / **ring** / el anillo / ayl ah-**nee**-yoh

roof / **roof** or **ruf** / el techo / ayl **tay**-shoh

sailboat / **sayl**-boht / el velero, el barco de vela / ayl vay-**lay**-roh, ayl **bahr**-koh day **vay**-lah

signs / **sines** / las señales / lahs say-**nyah**-lays

soccer ball / **sok**-ur **bawl** / el balón de fútbol, la pelota de fútbol / ayl bah-**lohn** day **foot**-bohl, lah pay-**loh**-tah day **foot**-bohl

starfish / **star**-fish / la estrella de mar / lah ays-**tray**-yah day mahr

stop sign / **stop sine** / la señal de alto / lah say-**nyahl** day **ahl**-toh

strawberries / **straw**-ber-eez / las fresas / lahs **fray**-sahs

suitcase / **soot**-kayss / la maleta / lah mah-**lay**-tah

tiles / **tiles** / las baldosas / lahs bahl-**doh**-sahs

tire / **tire** / la llanta / lah **yahn**-tah

traffic light / **traf**-ik **lite** / el semáforo / ayl say-**mah**-foh-roh

tray / **tray** / el charola, la bandeja / lah shah-**roh**-lah, lah bahn-**day**-hah

tree / **tree** / el árbol / ayl **ahr**-bohl

triangle / **trye**-ang-guhl / el triángulo / ayl tree-**ahn**-goo-loh

T-shirt / **tee**-shurt / la camiseta / lah kah-mee-**say**-tah

window / **win**-doh / la ventana / lah vayn-**tah**-nah

yarn / **yarn** / el hilo, la lana, el estambre / ayl **ee**-loh, lah **lah**-nah, ayl ays-**tahm**-bray